Unseasoned campaigner

Primitive
the call
of the word.

—DINAH HAWKEN, 'Stone'

Unseasoned campaigner

Janet Newman

OTAGO UNIVERSITY PRESS
Te Whare Tā o Te Wānanga o Ōtākou

Published by Otago University Press
Te Whare Tā o Te Wānanga o Ōtākou
533 Castle Street
Dunedin, New Zealand
university.press@otago.ac.nz
www.otago.ac.nz/press

First published 2021

ISBN 978-1-99-004810-4

Editor: Anna Hodge
Cover photograph: Shutterstock

Printed in New Zealand by Ligare

In memory of my parents

Contents

II. *Tender*

1. *How now?*

Drenching

When the cattle come from the saleyards
in the blue truck that clatters up the drive
they walk as in a daze. Some snatch at grass
glancing through cracks in the concrete.

Drench them now while they amble
easily into the race. Tomorrow,
stomachs full, they will gallop away
because you are a stranger to them

though in months, as each day
you open gates to paddocks
of fresh grass and in winter lay hay
on the ground before them,

they come, warm breath on your skin.
See them paw the soft peat,
worry the old scents where you buried
the drowned steer two winters past.

Until you send them on their way
to be killed, they grant the grace
of their company, draw you in with flared nostrils
that pause over the bones of their dead.

In the auction room

of the sale yards
as the Charolais mob below,
the men, mostly men, nod
or raise a finger to bid
the way a diner
raises a finger
to ask the waiter
for the bill.

Calf sale

The veal man shoos
the four-day-olds,

legs too long for long bodies,
hoofs still soft, turned in to ease
their coming out of their mothers,

searching with strong snouts
for mammal warmth the way
a human baby turns her open
mouth towards the breast.

I buy four. Three follow
my moving fingers to the trailer,
suck air through rolled tongues,
the last bundled in my arms.

The veal man herds his
into the truck with the high
steel sides.

Another steel-grey
truck on the road.
Inside, unseen cargo
turning their heads in the dark.

Although I have no reason to
I feel superior driving my calves
to paddocks of plump grass
nursing their plain orphan hunger.

How now?

Afternoon, I stop on the causeway, watch
a herd of Friesians, five, maybe six hundred,
cross the floodplain—a slow, black train.

Milkers on farm bikes. In my dad's day,
dairy farmers were called cow cockies,
a name you don't hear any more.

His Jerseys were a different breed:
brown cows of elocution lines,
nursery rhymes. Each had a name

starting every year with the next letter
of the alphabet. Ada the eldest,
Happy to Melanie my six pet calves.

Mum wrote the names on the sheet
for the herd tester and she, always a she,
spun the milk and stayed the night.

These high-boned Friesians flap barcodes
on yellow ear-tags. One neighbour calls
all his half thousand Sweetie.

It was a game, choosing names for cows.
How some would come to be pronounced
at the tea table: the kicker, the tail swatter …
                    I am getting to something

bigger than nostalgia. Those Jerseys I recall.
This long line of Friesians. Their hoofs
lay down already fading scrawls.

The rig

has a bull's neck,
is twice the weight
of the steers in his mob.

Half-castrated, the testicle retained
in his abdominal cavity
is secreting hormones.

His blushed penis
juts from the sheath.

The day I send him to slaughter
he guides three steers
up the ramp. The truck

has been improperly configured,
metal stairs must be extended,
animals reloaded.

Wiser now, educated
to the cramped chamber,
unaware his life and death

shadow a series of blunders,
he breaks two galvanised gates,
chases up the rails the drafter

who energises his electric prod,
vows to *get rid of that attitude*,
the testosterone pounding.

Undertone

The heifer is used to being touched
here, the vet says, pushing the half-metre-long

plastic probe between her labia.
Static whitens the screen.

A dark, liquid orb
cradles milky lightness.

The young cow stands motionless
until the boy extends his small hand

towards her gently dimpled nose.
She yanks away, bashes her soft neck into steel rails.

Good intentions

We live in an age of unintended consequences.
—Ulrich Beck, *World Risk Society*

1. Trickle down

Father said farming was in my bones.
He hacked the gorse that stained the flank of the hill,

steel blade striking stalks like stone.
I poisoned it. Summers, barbed bushes blunted, fell,

plots of dead grass collateral damage. Offspring grew sharp
until last year the slope was flush as a side of lamb.

In the crease of the gully where run-off swilled,
the old kahikatea rooted beyond the fenced reserve

—unshorn sheep once packed its pool of shade—
stands tall, leafless, lichen white, skeletal.

2. Enough

The four-day-old calf
is soaked in diarrhoea,
too weak to suck.

Tired, careless, I push
the tube down its throat,
funnel the liquid in.

Next day, its body
lies flat as shadow
on the woodchips,

nostrils cochineal
with electrolyte flooded
from stomach to lungs.

I will say it died the way
calves wrenched off their mothers
sometimes do,

telling the truth of things,
knowing the difference
between enough and too much.

3. Oh! Kee-o kee-o

Last night, cutting potatoes,
butterflying chicken. A hawk
framed itself in my kitchen window,
its gentle rocking glide
interspersed with lazy wing beats
so easy it was difficult to recall
that it was hunting for carrion
not flying freer than I felt
hovering over my chopping board,

the way next morning I was framed
in the windscreen
behind the steering wheel
hurrying to work
and another hawk—or perhaps the same hawk—
gripping road kill, slow to gain traction
in air without height, hefting the possum
with wing beats
inaudible above the clamour
of the engine and Radio New Zealand's
9am bird which unbelievably,
I thought afterwards,
was the mating
kee-o kee-o
of the swamp harrier,
a sound nothing like
the dumb thump
against the bumper.

Drought, Horowhenua

1.

The hungry cows
have been standing at the gate
all day. Every time I go outside

they follow along the fence line.
They don't know they are not mine.
They do know I am human. Some

are feeding calves. Every night
when I was breastfeeding
I ate bread with tea.

2.

Yesterday, the Ōhau River hit trigger point.
Level three water restrictions:
irrigators off, sprinklers banned,
gardens watered Tuesday and Thursday

7 to 9pm, swimming pools filled
with written permission, hosing
of paved areas prohibited
except in an emergency.

Consider: in Cape Town, Theewaterskloof Dam
is drying up. At Day Zero, the city's taps
will go dry. Water will be collected

from designated places. Will it be patrolled
by armed guards? Will there be a black
market in water, a market in grey water?

What if you spill your water?
Someone steals your water?

The water thief goes to jail,
receives water but you have none

which triggers the release of a bullet

that triggers bleeding

onto the pavement

washed down with a hose.

3.

The depth of the drain
is surprising, visible now,
empty sides flush with
regenerating bracken fern.

Stand with silt
sticking to boot soles,
up to your armpits in fingers
of Yorkshire fog,

a last cavern of coolness
on ancient dunes
where English grasses
have given up. How do the pines

retain their dizzy black, the conifers
their rowdy yellow in this
hollowing heat
intense as migraine?

Even the rushes
and Scotch thistles cling
to colour, though the dunes
are gaunt, ghostly,

sand slouching the way
skin hugged the corpse
of the miscarried calf
until bones gave in.

4.

It's like some kind of transfiguration
how Hebe Great Barrier Island
has turned green overnight
—the way transfused blood
pinkens anaemic skin—
each concave leaf
plump, sated with life-shine
not pale, drab, limp as I found
it yesterday covered in leaves
drained of life. Hebe Ruby, however,
has not responded to my watering,
hand-delivered by bucket
because the hose will not reach
these outliers situated
for their so-called hardiness.
Walking back to the house
beside ancient dunes
farmed for more than a century
I pass *Acer palmatum*, aka Bloodgood,
which has yielded to early summer heat
with bold autumn red.

5.

Overhead, the skylark calls
and you wonder if it is always
this loud, this solitary,

or just because the brown bird is stark
against a sky so blue and hard
you could skate on it.

We are in a holding pattern,
those of us rooted deeply here:
the tōtara, the bottlebrush,

the high-flying skylark.
It tilts and turns, creating contour
in a sky without relief.

Have a plan or you feel like you are losing control

Shift the horses in the evening
when it is cooler.

Leave the gates open
so they can find shade.

Know there may be nibbles
along fence lines, in dips.

Make sure they have plenty
of water.

Let them become resigned
to not moving around much,

drinking
and not eating

the way Aunty Joyce
accepted the sip cup

every hour but sometimes
could not swallow

and Uncle Maitland said if she was a horse
they would shoot her.

Elegy

The kingfisher calls for rain
but the rain does not come

although clouds gather
over the Tararuas,

promise the coming
of rain but the promised rain

doesn't come
so the soil cracks

and hardens beneath
clouds black as broken

promises that blacken
the broken eye of the lagoon

that looks for the kingfisher
but the kingfisher does not come.

Sponge and slate

The countryside has been transformed
from a sponge to a slate.

—HERBERT GUTHRIE-SMITH,
Tutira: The story of a New Zealand sheep station

Granny Smiths' skins
repel tap water
in my kitchen sink
as the shed's roof
sloughs the rain off
beside the broken guttering.
It has been coming down all day,
cut channels in the hard green skin
of the hills. Up north,
a farmer has videoed
a hillside sliding
like slate off a roof,
breaking in on itself
at the seat of the gully
where a flash stream
scours the tin pan plain.
The sudden current
dissolves the earth
like the brown sugar
in my bowl,
hoses the lax batter
into the risen river.

The apples are cooked to a pulp
beneath the sponge absorbing
juices, percolating flavour.

I dig my spoon into the pudding
topped with a scoop of ice cream,
watch the country melting.

Unseasoned campaigner

Winter

'Next year I'll be ready,' I say,
splinting my shin on the shovelhead,
jarring the blade on clay hard as tundra.

'I've heard that before,' says Winter.
Takes a drag on a cigarillo,
looks moonward.

'I'll have rye, fat and juicy, up to here,'
I say, tapping my thigh, throwing
another carcass into the pit.

He mocks with a cough, flips the butt
at an emaciated ewe, shifts
his weight to the other hip.

'Toodle-oo for now,' he says,
swivelling boot heels,
looking fit to skate on ice.

I sink to the shovel,
cover the corpses
with clay and gravel.

Spring

Three old man pines uprooted
across the back boundary, two
steers dead in a slip, the main drain

flooding the pump shed. Wind
circles the house. Another
tree down. The power goes out.

Spring, in the garden wearing
sensible shoes, brushes soil
from her gloves, flourishes

a phone gallery: daffodils,
new-born lambs. 'I planted
red cabbage, gold kūmara

and scarlet runner beans
before the rain,' she says,
cultivating a colourful grin.

Summer

The day I cut the willow trees down
because there is nothing else for the ewes to eat—

eyes stuck with dirt, udders empty, lambs
wrinkled as dried fruit—

Summer comes over the hill driving
a water tanker, a sheet of dust flapping behind.

I know it is her because last night when
the DOC hydrologist pronounced the river dead

she told me her name and sighed
when I said, 'That used to mean a good time.'

Water blows through the pipe, fills the tank
in a rush. 'This one's on me,' she says.

I hold her measured gaze when she warns,
'But it won't last with all these sheep.'

She leaves like the land, at once
generous and unforgiving.

Autumn

sits on a grass hump unlacing her boots.
Lank socks detach from elegant white feet,

toenails varnished ruby.
I look towards the dam.

A duck deadstick lands. Crackle
of webbed feet through water.

Her shirt hangs over raupō, jeans
a denim puddle, a cocksfoot

seed-head buffs the belt buckle.
She steps into the shallows.

Her face ripples like water.
She is a white shadow

beneath the dark lid, breasts
dusky fish. Shedding my clothes,

I slide into a blanket of cold.
On the bank, sun warms our skin,

tussock tickles bare limbs. Rye
ruffles the paddocks. Like us,

the grass is having one last flutter
before the long withdrawal.

The huntaway

lays his head in my lap
like a human child.
I rest my hand on loose pelt
coated in hair soft
as the head of a new-born,
wrap my palm around muzzle
that all morning scoured the ground
for scent of rabbit, stroke whiskers
that mapped the contours of burrows,
run my fingers along teeth that today
crunched the skulls of kits
snatched from subterranean nests.
My hand in his mouth
as in the steel jaws of a trap
set for the lightest footfall
rests like a host
on the heat of his tongue.
I have taken him
from his wild nest.
His wildness gives in,
he bows down,
receives my deviant touch,
gives to me his whole life
and I take it
as easily as I take food
from my plate to my mouth.

Suddenly rabbit

in seeded grass and summer thistledown,
the huntaway bounding behind.

(Yesterday he crushed a frail skull,
ate red flesh, ropey entrails.)

Tawny body, silent, swift.
The dog galumphs behind.

Neither slows and it seems
time slows and by slowing

lengthens as the chase extends surely beyond
the endurance of either.

The rabbit runs towards me,
all eyes and flattened ears

golden against the grass.
This one wild thing, no bigger

than a slipper. I think of its small
ribcage, leg bones no thicker

than my fingers,
heart a red bean.

It disappears beneath
the row of willows

into some dark, meandering burrow
where ardent kits suckle.

The carrier

His eyes under a creased cotton cap
don't give up much or give in, steeled
to the clop of hoofs, ease
of tonnages through yardings so narrow
wooden planks billow against hides.

He gentles them with low murmurings,
a father soothing a nightmared son:
Easy now, big boy. They walk toward
imagined fields, his voice lulling
them forward. He carries them to slaughter.

He's crisscrossed seas behind the wheel,
cab a jar of amber heat, musk of warm
payload. When they see him they are not
afraid: a measured gait, sidelong glance,
quietness—could be kindred.

The shearer

arrives in a dented Datsun,
ties the portable unit to a post
with electric-blue baling twine,
bundles the ewe against her crotch.

The wool is grey and stuck with docks
but when she shears it falls away
like taking off a robe. Underneath
is cream that gilded in sun looks gold.

Her arms, varnished with lanolin,
shine as under lights. The ewe's skin
is pink and flushed. Graceful,
their limbs and torsos entwine

until the lulling background buzz
of the handpiece ends. She unbends
as from a bow, pitches the gear
in the car like sacks of wheat,

drives across the ruts, the only
remembrance of their fleeting dance
the golden fleece, froth of lace
and tulle, bobbing on the back seat.

Meat processing plant poem 1: slaughterers

1.

The steers stand in the concrete yards
resting one leg and then another.
They receive water. Remnants
of first winter coats lift from their backs,
morning mist from lowland paddocks.

When the dogs bark and the drafter
claps a long stick against the rails
they walk obediently, single file, up
the ramp into the electric head bail, drop
to the white-walled room where the slaughterers work.

2.

One cuts the tender throats.
One hauls the chain.
One sharpens the knife.
One spools the rope.

Each washes the blood
off a white apron,
white boots and hands

in the windowless room
from spring to autumn
where the only prayer
is the shush of water.

Meat processing plant poem II: not snow

There is nothing
familiar here, nothing

resembling leaf, stone,
cloud as mist over home

paddocks although it's white
and cold. No light

but neon. In wide
corridors, torsos slide

on ceiling tracks,
muscle-bound, sheathed in fat.

Wearing white overalls, white hats,
men push vats

of guts,
hearts like knots.

Cherry-ripe blood
spreads a hot-embered flood

over the drained-of-colour floor
that is as white as nothing at all.

Ode to *Mycoplasma bovis*

In the drifting rain the cows in the yard are as black
And wet and shiny as rocks in an ebbing tide

       —RUTH DALLAS, 'Milking Before Dawn'

Your name fills the mouth
as you fill the cows' lungs with lesions.

You were everywhere except
this 'pure' place, now here you are

with your *multifactorial pathogenicity*,
your *exposed membrane proteins*.

You enter ears easier than those sounds,
make them stagger, fall,

brown their milk.
O, how you sneak in through

the letterbox flap, slide smooth
and streamlined right up

their cunts in semen straws,
frozen embryos

we bred for resilience.
You sire millions.

Anti-pastoral: Biosecurity Act 1993, section 130

But they smell of the soil, as leaves lying under trees
Smell of the soil, damp and steaming, warm.

—Ruth Dallas, 'Milking Before Dawn'

This is a restricted place.

Wash hands, soles of boots.

Drive through a disinfectant bath.

Sluice flat decks with Virkon.

Wear personal protective clothing (PPC).

Although you may be tempted

by the sight of romping calves,

their warm coats, earthy scents,

do not approach. On entry,

report to the farm manager.

Observe electric wires

each side of the boundary fence

to keep neighbouring cows at least two metres apart

to ensure there is no touching,

no nose to nose contact,

no exchange of breath.

Singular steer

with strength to suck
    the rings
off my fingers at
    four days old,
shoulders through steel
    head bail.
Forelegs crease to concrete,
    hindquarters
catch in high rail as a
    carcass raised
to the meat hook.

From walking plank,
    I pour endectocide
withers through tailhead
    to kill hookworm,
wireworm, mange,
    nits, lice.
Wait for him to right.
    He stills.
Lips merge a puddle
    of dribble.

Five times my weight, all
    bone and muscle,
head hard as an anvil. Hard
    to move.
(I recall dragging a steer
    from the drain
with a sling rigged from
    tow rope.)

Hoofs lethal. A minute
        goes by,
another. Blood rosies the rails.

I could say
        he is accustomed
to pain, wrenched from warm
        udder, mothered
to Peach Teats, borne
        dehorning
iron, castration ring.

I could say
        he declined
the yank of that rope
        around his throat.

All I know is he
        kicked through,
shuddered up,
        sauntered off,
his moment of singular
        cattleness lost
to mob blur, din and heat
        of the yards.

II. *Tender*

Tender

When my father said the rabbit
was tough my mother promised
to boil it longer,
a shame to waste good meat.
He told my sister it was chicken,
said our pet lambs
went back to their mothers.

Every time he found a burrow
he tramped to the shed
for the spade, a length of chicken wire,
swearing like a sergeant.
He would always come in
from the paddocks
shouldering the shovel or grubber

except the day he lifted from his pocket
the kit spared from the hay mower
by his Geneva Convention
and held it out to me in cupped palms
as trembling proof of his boyhood.

Talking to my father

Most people called him Doug
and he did,

held a shovel as though
it was a spoon,

bowl blade
worn as a mouth.

Tree holes, post holes, drains,
a swimming pool,

graves for chooks, dogs, calves.
Trenches.

To cut square edges
he used a spade,

called it
a spade.

Dehorning the calves

Most went willingly into the crate,
urged by my father's voice.

Head-to-tail down the narrow race,
slight bodies crushed
between wooden boards,
noses manacled with elastic rope,

the hot iron bit into their heads.

My stomach tensed as their spines arched,
legs seized, mouths fell open
retching tongues white as ghosts.
Shocked, guttural groans.

The shed stank
of scorched hair and burnt flesh.

Every year, one or two could not bear it.
Limbs flailed
against steel rails, bodies
bruised on concrete.

My father called them the wild ones,
spirited, hard to handle,

the way he called me
rebellious before I left
then independent afterwards

his voice closer to admiration
than rebuke.

Man of few words

He picks over uneven ground for footings
in puddles, pug-holes,

passes lines of macrocarpa broken
by blank spaces where the westerly tore through.

His language is electric rhythm of pump and wire,
gush of couplets from the artesian bore,

a flighty heifer enjambed
with a low rail,

stanza of cloud over the back paddock
threatening rain,

the *fuck, fuck, fuck*
of a dead bull in the drain.

This life

He checks each hairy ear
for a barcode, considers
the roundness of rumps,

urges them up the ramp
with warm milk words,

uses protective electric shock
to prod them into smaller
and smaller
spaces.

His voice grows loud
above the clang of bodies
in the truck's metal chamber.

He hoses out the yard, tries
to wash the dirt away,

puts mineral blocks
beside troughs
for those that remain.

They lick the proffered salt
the way their mothers

licked them into this life
with rough tongues.

Parade ground

He told us to yank off sticking plasters,
let the air get to it
his anthem for any wound;
said his mates laughed
through dysentery, bed bugs, hunger,
the corpses absent from his yarns

though he banned guns from the toy box
and *I'll kill you* shouted
when one sister drank the other's fizz.
Kill was for the cat's mouse,
the mutton sheep.

When on the evening TV news
the Vietnam War boomed,
his cheeks filled red and round
as poppies, his words wilted
our petal ears, hung like ghosts
with all the dead in the living room.

Tinnitus

He rode the mail truck
to school, bare feet surfing
the running board, one arm

flapping. Flying,
he was lighter than air,
lighter even than light.

At Monte Cassino
the sky was black with planes.
He never really listened

or stoppered his ears. Walking
through rye and clover, spray gun
sweeping left, right, left,

backpack warning:
ACHTUNG Schutzkleidung tragen
(DANGER Wear protective clothing).

Sometimes, he could hear
the grass breathe
between the roaring.

Gunner

He said you had to make sure you were standing right or the kickback would dislocate your shoulder. They weren't given earmuffs or told to put their fingers in their ears. He and Tom stood and waited while the gun roared and echoed. Later, he heard the roaring and echoing inside his head all night long. Mother took to using a high-pitched shriek and in moments of clarity he'd shout: 'Do you think I'm deaf?'

On pie day

Mother dusted the kitchen table white,
weighed half a pound of flour in the silver dish

(a nugget of lead the counterbalance)
a splash of water from the enamel mug

stirred to a pale skin. Half a pound of butter
chopped in knobs, pressed with the wooden pin

until bright streaks merged like golden zippers.
The fat flesh folded neat as a napkin,

laid to rest on the rack in the fridge.
After lunch, the tablecloth swept away,

the green Formica powdered again,
she rolled the cold mound

until blisters of air bobbed inside flabby folds.
About the house we mouthed the promised crust,

senses tuned to tremor of the table leg,
murmur of the rolling pin,

reach of her bare arms, slow stretch of dough,
the sure way the air was caught.

Praises

The priest said there was a time
to die, a time to plant and grow, a time
to live, a righteous way, a place, a path
and other things I forget.

The daughter said the life was long,
good things were done when she
was young: black hair, dark eyes,
red lips always smiling.

The only one who brought the man-spirit
back to the grieving husband
was the nephew from Hokitika
riding a black Harley-Davidson,

chrome grille,
fins elegantly bent,
stories of street races,
sand-blasted beaches,

who lifted the silver bonnet
on the new model Holden sedan
and sang the praises
of its straight-six four-litre donk.

His bones

The x-rays show
my father's bones
are wearing thin,
eroding like the
sandstone pinnacles
at Cervantes.
Each year a little
rubs off until
they're thin columns
weathered more
in some places
than others,
silted away at elbows,
knees and hips
till sockets scrape
against flattened joints.

When he walks
it is with an awkward,
angular gait
like a cupboard
that opens askew
when the hinges
are not fixed
in the right places.

Post-op

I brought a dozen Speight's
in one hand,
his away-from-home bag
in the other.

The surgeon pulled me aside:
How often does he drink? And how much?

Hmm …

at the end of the day,
the grubber angled against the shed,
he has a beer,

after harrowing
in the spring sun,

once the hay is pressed and stacked,
the lemon drink drunk,

after burying the steer drowned in the drain,
dragged by the leg with the tractor and chain
to a hole dug with a shovel.

At Christmas
he has a shout

when Max from down the road calls in
or Uncle Tim comes by to talk the war out

or late at night
when only he and I are up
and stories: *Trieste* ...
wine in barrels
... Monte Cassino ...
purple death ...

and now this job is done.

Sixty years

It was the first time I had seen him cry. I was so taken aback I could not look away, even though I knew I was intruding into a private space where I had no business being. I stared and stared at his red, glassy eyes trying to hide under his great paw of a hand. He was shading them as if from the glare of the sun or the stare of my eyes transfixed by this show of such ordinary humanness. The only sound was my breath, not even the tick of a clock, just my breath and his silent crying in the kitchen where he sat in his low-slung chair and me beside him on the couch, breathing slow and loud. He was my mother's hard man, the belt-behind-the-kitchen-door man. All I could think was the memory was old and sixty years must have gone so fast.

And in a moment

He didn't tell me to slow down,
just put one hand on the dash
like he was ready for anything.

Soon we were where the grass grew
rough, the gateways were brown
and the only grey was the road.

He gestured with his thumb.
Grass seeds tickled the exhaust
and sang as we drove up the hill.

'Here'll do,' he said, and got out
of the car without looking around
or straightening his back.

Six slow strides to the fence
as though he'd spent the whole morning
walking to reach this high ground.

He rested his hand on the top wire,
shifted his weight—battens
creaked, took the strain—as though

waiting to whistle up the dog
to bring the herd over the hill
and in a moment you'd see

the tangle of hoofs, brown legs
heaving swaying udders up the track.
He'd latch the gate, walk to the yard,

hear the milking machine humming
to a slow classical song on the wireless
bolted over the middle bail.

He didn't seem to notice the barb
puncturing his skin, the drop of red
on the grass going grey in the dusk.

Stepping stones

For months, he kept her ashes
beside their bed. In July, woke early
before light or winter birdsong, windows wet,
went outside in warm pyjamas, gumboots, a beanie.
Each step crushed frosted grass. Took the urn
to the garden where she fell, spread an outline
like a crime scene. Ash or bone wedged
in his boot tread, crunched on steps. Specks
appeared beside the sink. Next day and the next,
he walked between house and garden, each footfall
falling in a footprint, each step forward stepping back.

Drought

After mother died, father said
he'd get used to living alone
the way rye grass in his paddocks gets by

without rain.

Obliteration

The family favourite tree—
maroon plums she
preserved behind glass

or laid in velvet trifles—
leaves a pale sawdust stain
on the grass.

Where her red shavers
sang shanty songs
over breakfast eggs

with marigold yolks
and whites white
as fresh milk junket

sounds the flap
of a thrush trapped
behind mesh.

The drawers are stuffed
with embroidered cloths,
doilies—pinks, violas—

with the long hours
her fingers wove
with shuttle, needles, hook.

He lays a newspaper
on the dining table,
eats from a pot on his lap,

his body listing
in the billowing chair,
the TV always on,

the unfathomable remote
caught in a crag.
Lone as a boy

untwinned,
he wills the sea to flood in,
would drown if he could.

Father's funeral

It was that day we mowed and pruned,
sprayed the dog with the hose,
filled the heap with fresh clippings
and you didn't come to the end of the garden
by the old glasshouse to prime the mower
like you always did in your thick boots
and gruff voice. You stayed inside
while the mower whirred and chopped
and the dog yelped. When the day came
to a sudden close with spatters of rain
on the west window, you didn't move,
didn't toss a bone through the wire kennel
with a soft 'tucker time', didn't follow us
down the concrete path to the car, a sugar sack
of new potatoes you grew behind the slat fence
clenched in one fist, a plastic bag of beans
picked this morning, dappled with condensed
dew, swinging loosely in the other. As the car
circled the paddock we didn't see you leaning
against the corrugated corner of the shed, one leg
bent across the other like a soldier waiting
by the flap door of the mess tent
or one arm raise up when you turned for the gate
as if stretching for that apple with the red blush
just within reach of the top rung.

That day, you stayed in the chair by the fire, head
down, dozing, your back to the world as it spun,
you at the centre, the rest turning around.

Next day

Beige corduroy slippers
toe by toe on the mat,

that darned green jersey
over the head of the La-Z-boy.

On the path,
the red stain where he fell.

The sun lightens it and the same wind
is noisy in the pear tree.

The undertaker gave me

In the office on Queen Street East
the undertaker gave me a white envelope
the weight of a handful of stones.
His watch: a folded silver
crescent, a moon without a sky.
I held it in my hand into the dim chapel.
I saw my father—as much like my father
as anything else—shoulders back, nose
pointing skyward, his face a perfect calm,
arms by his sides at parade rest, the skin
below his cuffs weathered, around
his left wrist the bright white band.

Digging

All winter he had dug, boot
against the shovelhead slicing
frozen orchard clay, shouldering
the barrow up the ramp while I
read in the fire-warmed lounge
and mourned the lost Gravenstein.

Years later, worried city-born
grandchildren might drown, he hitched
the trailer, mined sixteen loads
of clay from the cow track's
north face and four of peat
for Christmas potatoes to dangle in.

Today, the children, half-grown,
wait beneath the rostrum
while I take my place,
lift one-sixth of his weight,
consider the unexpected things:

the lightness of him,
how I came to be
the one to decide
where to dig
and when to fill in.

Father's beanie

Limp as
a shot hare,

pilled, frayed,
oil-stained brim,

loose ends
of stitch.

III. *Ruahine*

Stilts

I am hot, alone in paddocks
baked hard by drought.
My father is dead.

I see him shovelling clay into the trailer.
The stubble on his chin
is as sharp as pine needles.
Sweat wets the furrows
of his brow.
It is time to go in.
I raise my right arm above my head,
nestle my hand
in his rough palm.
A cool breeze blows
through our shirts.

He is guiding the screaming saw
through the plank.
Black hairs finger the neck
of his singlet.
He wraps long arms around the poles,
grips the pegs with bare toes.

Diesel

after Ian Wedde

When I wrap my hand around the wooden handle of the pump
    screwed onto the 44-gallon drum—

When I wrap my hand around the oval handle,
    pull it out and push it down—

When I wrap my hand around the familiar handle
    and let it rise up inside my palm

I hear the gurgle of diesel deep inside. I feel
    resistance as it sucks into the pipe.

When I wrap my hand around the wooden handle
    smoothed by my father's palm,

I hold the tin bucket in my left hand as he did in his right,
    the wire handle caught inside my fist,

fingers rolled inside my palm, thumb across knuckles
    (*don't put your thumb inside or it will break when you
    punch*),

wire cutting into the creases of my joints, diesel gushing
    from the metal spout, catching the air

as when a cow arches her spine to piss and the urine blows back
    against her udder and the backs of her legs.

When I climb onto the tractor, one foot on the gridded
    metal footrest, the other on the steering rod,

lift the bucket over the funnel pouring the diesel
    into the wide metal mouth

until the bucket lightens and I upend it
    to slide out the last oily drops,

I am watching from the concrete floor, standing beside
    the T-bone tread

of the rear tyre, taller than me, that smells
    of smoke and rubber.

This is the last drum and when it is empty the tanker driver
    will no longer point his electric nozzle

into the hole in the top, screw on the cap,
    help my father roll it

across the concrete yard to the back of the cowshed,
    sheltered from rain and wind.

Rural Fuel has declared the custom unsafe and uneconomic.
    Instead, I will fill a yellow plastic can

at the bowser in town. The drum, the metal pump
    with its worn wooden handle, the funnel

and the tin bucket coated in a fine film of fragrant diesel
    will stay tucked in the warm comfort of the shed.

There comes a time

to cut down the last windbreak macrocarpa,
trunk embedded with wire and the staples

he hammered in. He put an orange
in my stocking every year—ghosts

of his boyhood without. After Mum died
he was a ghost of himself. But I digress.

Straining that fence he was at his best—
sure as a stay, strong as wind, straight

to the point, his anger
casual as a handshake.

When he slit a sheep's throat
he skewed its neck against bare shins.

He took me to Seed & Grain Co.
in my mini dress to drink beer

with men on hay bales, sent me
down the cattle track

where cold wind cradled my skin,
said 'don't let it beat you'

as though standing unflinching
was enough to stop a steer

ten times my weight.
And it was.

Preserving

Red plums give up
round plump bodies
when I cut out their stones.
I hear my mother's long-ago voice:
'Don't overdo it.' The boiling
and much else. In the photograph
she is smiling behind glass, my memory
of her steeped in absence. Now,
even that faithless call sounds sweet
as in preserving jars sour plums
surrender to sugar syrup.

Weeds

Again, I lumber down the track
on my blood-red quad bike
with my mustard-yellow spray pack

past the old seat
where six years ago
I spread my father's remains

resembling not so much ashes
as the fertiliser grains
he spread each autumn.

Summers, he marched down this track
with his grubber
to hew out Californian thistles.

Americans call them Canadian thistles,
the British call them cursed thistle,
lettuce from Hell.

Grandmother called him
Clemenceau after the 1919
Paris Peace Conference.

Twenty-three years later,
he was an anti-tank gunner
at Monte Cassino.

I remember the names
he called the TV
when the wars were on the news.

He was a soldier named for a peacemaker,
for hope that keeps pushing through
like rye and clover.

Hammer

See the cold steel weathered toolshed grey, diesel
damp, dull as stone. Impenetrable. See the weight.

Snub nose roughly round, claws bared, leather-brown
stump wedged, streaked with sweat. Alien

as the woodwork room: boys slouched over slant desks,
sawdust and dust as you passed down the hall.

See instead the gentle scroll, polished stem, smooth
as bone. Wrap your hand around. Pick it up, feel

its scope, head poised above your fulcrum wrist. Swing it,
let its weight drive it down. Tilt your arm, site your feet.

Pinch the staple. Tap. Shift the angle the way you would
your pen to write, lips to speak. Find the fine point.

Own it, soften it. Wield the age-old club. The barbs
pierce the post. The pine opens to your blows.

At the floodplain farm

Not I, some child, born in a marvellous year,
Will learn the trick of standing upright here.

—ALLEN CURNOW, 'The Skeleton of the Great Moa
in Canterbury Museum, Christchurch'

The ground shudders
as cattle trample past.

Peat sinks around perimeters
of kahikatea stumps

gouged by hoofs.
I could lie inside

their soft centres.
Roots thick as limbs

dredged by the digger
bleach like bones in the sun.

A pūkeko strides
towards the shelterless drain

white tail feathers
buffeted by wind.

This easy sea of grass
steams with sweat.

After the Wairau Affray
and the 1855 earthquake,

Paiaka settlers abandoned
the riverbank mill, moved

downstream to Te Awahou
or bought farm allotments.

South to Hōkio
they named Mt Robinson block.

With handsaw, shovel and axe
they 'broke it in',

learnt the trick of cross-sawing
the patient trunks,

dragged them out
with bullock team and jigger board,

heard tūī, kererū, tīeke
sounding through the canopy

of marvellous kahikatea
that stood upright here.

All afternoon

high branch
blue gum
tūī peals

bells
       bells

low branch
kahikatea
chainsaw drones

on and
       on and

bird
    saw
saw
      bird

never in tune
all the afternoons

Game: a pair of haiku

dawn the sixth of May
gunshots explode like blossom
a pair of mallards

each easy wing beat
unknowable as falling snow
pop

Cockerels

Today, five, feathers shining
as tinsel, and one dour brown hen,
rake sheep shit in the yards.

From the bush
beyond the grazed hill, a call
so familiar it seems native

to this fenced reserve
where discarded cockerels
and one hen mistaken for a cockerel

forge a flock. Pitiless,
they will fight
for the right to mate with her

in this patch
of rekindling kahikatea,
cautiously returning kererū, kākāriki.

They primp and scratch
like gaudy heroes, dislodge
grubs, seedlings.

Someone supposed
this was a natural place
to release the unwanted,

supposed it was the humane
not merely human
thing to do.

Animal

1. Supplication

Climb the boundary fence to walk the dogs.
The hungry cows barrel down the hill,
bellowing, calling you, human,
to release them
from the sand and dung
they have been standing on for days.
Hides cling to ribcages,
two hundred thin necks lean
into barbed wire.

2. Appreciation

The whale
tangled in old net
approaches the fishing boat
and when set free
by the hands
that may have snared it
rises out of the water
not once
but twice,
the sound
of its huge body
striking the sea.

3. Elation

Dusk.
Sunlight rims
ancient dunes,
gilds the coastal plain.
Smoke plumes from the bonfire,
adds substance to the thickening night.
Sparks fly as bright insects
into the extinguishing sky.
The huntaway circles
the fire, paws skidding
on short grass, turns,
runs the other way
around, returns.

Reading *Moby-Dick* the week of Peter Bethune's trial

Herman Melville has me rowing the longboat,
rope-end of the iron-honed, muscle-thrown harpoon.

On board *Pequod*, the enormous head is suspended by a block and
tackle.
Through a hole dug with a spade, those brave and ignorant men

dip an iron bucket 'precisely like a well bucket' again and again,
haul brimming, opaque, emollient jelly. It slops the deck.

They slide about like pucks. All the dumb night,
oil lamps burn bright.

Whales. I have seen the poise of their tails,
the dark arch of their backs from a boat off the Kaikōura coast.

YouTube camcorder: The calf nudges the kayak with its outlandish
snout.
Baby, we love you, sweet baby. A hand reaches out.

Google search: Anatomy of a sperm whale. Professor Malcolm
Clarke
beside a life-size diagram of a teenager the length of this room.

There's an oil network
delaying sound reception for sonar perception,

water-cooled, blood-warmed oil solidifies, liquefies,
allows the whale to rise and dive

with the grace of a locomotive-size dancer.
It's nature's brilliance.

Every night on the news, flukes first, white bellies up,
up the slips of smart whaling ships

and madman Bethune, a crossbow in one hand,
roaming the seas on their tails.

Beach

Some days the clouds disappear
on the drive to the coast

the way the things you wanted to say
evaporate when you get there.

Sentences float to the pencil-line horizon
between sky that is nothing but blue

and sea that is as blue as ...
but words fail you,

smudge like the fishing boats
in the distance without your binoculars

or the telescope mounted
in your absolutely beachfront window,

wash like driftwood
onto Kāpiti's stony shore

where gulls patrol for intruders
to absolutely beachfront nesting grounds,

drift to the Sounds, wrap around
mussel-farm ropes, catch in cray pots

or loll beneath the surface like snapper, gurnard
or closer in, in warmer water, kahawai swim out of reach.

Soon the miles of driftwood on the beach
look just like washed-up words,

the ones you wanted to use
pristine untrammelled calming

but found were of no use
although they seemed elegant

lying in your mind the way driftwood
shaped like big fish swimming reclines in gardens

but is truly uprooted trees
floated down the river, drained of colour,

pummelled until smooth
and left on the high-water line to dry

like the words you wanted to say,
jetsam on the tide.

Magpies on Koputaroa Road

Before long, you're around
the last bend, heading
towards the highway, past

the lone cabbage tree,
flower-head torn off
by the salt-laden westerly. I read

a kahikatea forest stabilised
the dunes, kept the wind at bay
when magpies were brought. They

sing their odd, untranslatable songs,
quardle, as poets say,
dawdle on warm tarseal. It pays

to ease off the throttle
as you swoop around
the corner, takes time

to rise in flight
and contrition's no use
to feathers on metal. It's hard

not to think even they
don't much chance.
So many cars, so few trees,

the only certain thing
the road, winging its way
across the plain.

Koputaroa, near the Manawatū River

Last night, mid-winter, a morepork
was in the naked silver birch, her ruru
like a bassoon player tuning up;
more a thickness than a sound,
a bar of acoustic colour against the thin
TV speak in our lounge.

Purple the Tararuas this morning
before they transmogrified
(there's a word to fill
the mouth like a boiled lolly,
primary coloured, white swirl,
twisted in clear cellophane
from Woolworths' pick 'n' mix
then McKenzies, then Kmart,
now $2 Dragon Market)
to turquoise, mauve
when the mist rises.

For eight hundred years or more,
Muaūpoko saw underfeathers lifting.
Kōpū-toroa: breast of an albatross.

Down the front steps,
my socked feet on the pebbled path,
the Milky Way bright in the quiet cold.
She sounded again and an answering call,
a flute an octave or two higher,
from the bottlebrush at the end of the drive.

I shone my torch into the leafless
branches and she stayed in my glare,
thirty centimetres or more tall,
motionless. My daughter, dressing
for a party, unappreciative
of my urging, poked her head
around the open door
then shut the chill outside.

Before bed, I went out again
but she was gone, the tree strangely bare
without her dark weight
inside its slender limbs. Penetrating stars
threatened frost. Suddenly cold,
I hurried in, heard my daughter's hasty 'bye',
car engine's rumble, discordant iPod beat
pitching percussion at the brittle night.

Empty nest

Pita, the white-faced heron, flies back
to the bird rescue centre each day
even though he's old enough
to be out in the wild, says Lyn—
who hand-reared him after his nest
blew over in a storm—
in the latest issue of *New Zealand*
Geographic. She thinks he has
a sight problem
but I read slight problem
and cannot see
how returning for an easy meal
is a problem, more a sign of intelligence
like the city pigeons on page nineteen
that have learnt to recognise four-letter words
from four jumbled letters
and to peck a screen for wheat
when the words appear. I wonder
what happens when the experiment ends?
Will they peck road signs
like Dead Slow or Tawa Left Lane
or were the words in the lab
more like the four-letter words
graffitied at my daughter's school
or on the Fire Exit sign she stole
and hung above her door
before she left for university
or her words I hunger for
each morning before breakfast,
tapping my phone.

Moby

never saw another sheep, hugged
the boundary, wore a path to sand,
grew familiar as that house or tree
you fail to see until struck by its absence.

Twelve shears. Each fleece a thick cloak,
underneath creamy as blubber. This year
a thinner coat and no struggle
with the shearer. She lay down

as though glad to rest from the day's chores:
grazing, chewing cud, limping to the trough
and back to shade, stomach concave, knees black
with scabs, rump red under a mat of maggots.

I found her beached under the kahikatea,
her good eye already clouded, spilled
water from the cup of my hand.
I had no gun. My son

was three when she was an orphan lamb.
He clung to my hair when we swam.
Each day he dives and breaches.
I swear, I never meant
to take a single one for granted.

To a daughter in London

If you could see

the seed potatoes
in a fresh-dug
trench, round

bottoms cupped
in dark, rain-
wet soil

streaked with lime
and potassium forked
through, eyes

seeking light
under light
blankets

of loam, soft-curled
leaves uncrumpling
over mounds,

how on the other side
of earth their
fierce hearts swell.

Ruahine

Poplars hold the steep slopes
at the tops of the foothills. I stop
to catch my breath. It's the view
that holds me here, low hills
around the old woman range
clutching the purple spill of her skirt.

The ridge I biked made me sweat.
All the way up, I felt regret for the lost forest.
From here, I'll wind the road down to the plain
then home to my partner making pizza for two,
the sparse dining table, vacant bedrooms
although I wouldn't be here without the road
or if my children hadn't grown.

I hike up the gears, pedal down
to the river and one-lane bridge. Even
loss has its own joy. To see the hills
across the bare land. To see them
raise up so strong and clear.

Acknowledgements

Thanks are due to the publishers and editors of the following publications in which some of these poems, sometimes in different forms, first appeared: *Across the Fingerboards*, *Atlanta Review New Zealand*, *Blackmail Press*, *Bravado*, *Ice Diver*, *Landfall*, *Manifesto Aotearoa: 101 political poems*, *New Zealand Poetry*, *Nth Degree*, *Penguin Days*, *Poetry New Zealand Yearbook*, *Scattered Feathers*, *Snorkel*, *Swamp*, *takahē* and *The Unexpected Greenness of Trees*.

I would like to acknowledge the significant contribution to my work of competitions, in which a number of these poems have been placed: Caselberg International Poetry Prize, IWW Kathleen Grattan Prize for a Sequence of Poems, New Zealand Poetry Society International Poetry Competition, Otago University Press Kathleen Grattan Poetry Award, *Poetry New Zealand* Poetry Prize, Still Waving Climate Change Creative Writing Competition and *takahē* Poetry Competition.

The sequence 'Drought, Horowhenua' contains found language from a Horowhenua District Council press release, 'Level 3 Water Restrictions are now in place for Levin' (8 December 2017); and lines four and five in 'Oh! Kee-o kee-o' are from New Zealand Birds Online. I also acknowledge two RNZ news reports by Conan Young, 'Cow cubicle dairy farm tested in Canterbury' (14 August 2017) and 'Bull semen likely culprit as M bovis origin—researcher' (29 March 2018), which inspired 'Ode to *Mycoplasma bovis*'.

I am grateful to Massey University for awarding me a Vice-Chancellor's Doctoral Scholarship in 2017–19, when many of these poems were written.

My very special thanks to Professor Bryan Walpert and Associate Professor Ingrid Horrocks for wise counsel and enduring encouragement over many years.

Thanks to fellow poets Johanna Aitchison and Margaret Moores who read and commented on many of these poems, offered peer support and invaluable friendship.

Thanks to Rachel Scott, formerly of Otago University Press, for accepting my manuscript and to the anonymous readers who helped me to make it better. Thanks to Anna Hodge for cheerful and rigorous editing. Many thanks to the OUP team: publisher Sue Wootton, designer Fiona Moffat and publicist Laura Hewson for being a pleasure to work with.

Very little would have been possible without the support and constancy of my family. Much love and thanks to Lyle, Wynton and Delia Newman, and to Frank Taylor, always.